History in Living Memory

Education
Through the Years

How Going to School
Has Changed in
Living Memory

Clare Lewis

heinemann raintree

To contact Capstone Global Library please
call 800-747-4992, or visit our web site
www.capstonepub.com

Edited by Clare Lewis and Holly Beaumont
Designed by Philippa Jenkins
Picture research by Tracy Cummins
Production by Victoria Fitzgerald
Originated by Capstone Global Library Ltd
Printed and bound in China by Leo Paper Group

18 17 16 15 14
10 9 8 7 6 5 4 3 2 1

Library of Congress Cataloging-in-Publication Data
Lewis, Clare, 1976-
   Education through the years : how going to school has changed in living memory / Clare Lewis.
      pages cm.—(History in living memory)
   Includes bibliographical references and index.
   ISBN 978-1-4846-0926-2 (hb)—ISBN 978-1-4846-0931-6 (pb)—ISBN 978-1-4846-0941-5 (ebook) 1. Education—United States—History. I. Title.

LA205.L48 2015
370.973—dc23   2014015495

This book has been officially leveled by using the F&P Text Level Gradient™ Leveling System.

Acknowledgments
We would like to thank the following for permission to reproduce photographs: Alamy: © Trinity Mirror/Mirrorpix, 15; Capstone Press: Philippa Jenkins, 1 Bottom Left, 1 Top Left; Corbis: © Bettmann, 14, © ClassicStock, 6; Getty Images: Bert Hardy, 7, Duane Howell/The Denver Post, 17, George Marks/Retrofile, 9, H. Armstrong Roberts, 8, Jacobsen/Three Lions, 11, Lambert, 10, Popperfoto, 13, T. Lanza/National Geographic, 16, Walter Sanders/Time Life Pictures, 12; Library of Congress: Lewis Wickes Hine, 4; Shutterstock: Carlos andre Santos, 23 Bottom, DJTaylor, 23 Middle, Everett Collection, Cover Top, Flas100, Design Element, Kollet, 23 Top, KUCO, 5 Top, Monkey Business Images, 20, 21, 22 Bottom, 22 Top Right, Pressmaster, 22 Top Left, Studio DMM Photography, Designs & Art, Design Element; SuperStock: Design Pics, Cover Bottom; Thinkstock: Big Cheese Photo, 18, Back Cover, Stockbyte, 19.

Every effort has been made to contact copyright holders of material reproduced in this book. Any omissions will be rectified in subsequent printings if notice is given to the publisher.

Some words are shown in bold, **like this**. You can find them in the glossary on page 23.

007154LEOS15

Contents

What Is History in Living Memory?

Some history happened a very long time ago. Nobody alive now lived through it.

Some history did not happen very long ago. Our parents, grandparents, and adult friends can tell us how life used to be. We call this history in living memory.

How Have Schools Changed in Living Memory?

When your grandparents were young, classrooms were not as bright and colorful as they are now.

Teachers were often very **strict** in the old days. Children had to work quietly and not talk to each other.

How Did Your Grandparents Get to School?

Getting to school was different from today. Not as many people had cars.

Most children walked or rode bikes to school. Children usually walked with their friends, not their parents.

How Were Classrooms Different in the 1950s?

In the 1950s, children sat at desks arranged in rows. The teacher usually stayed at the front of the classroom.

The teacher wrote on a **blackboard** in chalk. Children copied information down onto paper.

How Were Classes Different in the 1950s and 1960s?

When your grandparents were young, there were no computers. Children learned new ideas from books and from their teachers.

Girls and boys sometimes had different classes. Some girls learned sewing in school, while boys learned **woodworking**.

How Did Children Learn About the World?

Like today, students in the 1970s learned about other countries. They could watch television programs about them in school.

Some children had pen pals from around the world. They wrote letters to them to ask about life in their country.

What Was School Like in the 1980s?

Children sat in groups and worked together, instead of only listening to the teacher. The teacher moved around the classroom more, like today.

Computers started to be used in schools in the 1980s. Instead of writing only on paper, some children could now do their work on computers and print it out.

What Changed in the 1990s?

Many teachers started to use whiteboards in the 1990s. They are brighter than blackboards and less messy.

In the 1990s, children began to use the Internet in school. They could get information from people all over the world.

What Is Your School Like Today?

How do you learn in school today? Do you work alone or in groups with your classmates? Is your classroom fun and lively?

You can still learn a lot from books. Your teacher still helps you find things out. Now you can use interactive whiteboards and tablets in school, too.

Picture Quiz

Which of these was used in classrooms in the 1950s?

blackboard

interactive whiteboard

tablet

How is this different from the things you use today?

Picture Glossary

blackboard
dark board for writing on with chalk

strict
if someone is strict, he or she makes sure that rules are obeyed

woodworking
making things out of wood

Find Out More

Books

Hunter, Nick. *History Around You* (History at Home). Chicago: Heinemann Library, 2014.

Rissman, Rebecca. *Going to School* (Comparing Past and Present). Chicago: Heinemann Library, 2014.

Web site

FactHound offers a safe, fun way to find Internet sites related to this book. All of the sites on FactHound have been researched by our staff.

Here's all you do: Visit www.facthound.com
Type in this code: 9781484609262

Index